GREAT PICTURES
AND THEIR STORIES

How To Look At Pictures

"You must look at pictures studiously, earnestly, honestly. It will take years before you come to a full appreciation of art; but when at last you have it, you will be possessed of the purest, loftiest and most ennobling pleasures that the civilized world can offer you."

JOHN C. VAN DYKE.

ST.
A A
PRESS

GREAT PICTURES
AND THEIR STORIES

INTERPRETING
MASTERPIECES
TO CHILDREN

BY
KATHERINE MORRIS LESTER

BOOK THREE

ST. AUGUSTINE ACADEMY PRESS

This book was originally published in 1927
by Mentzer, Bush & Company.

This facsimile edition reprinted in 2024
with improved color images
by St. Augustine Academy Press.

ISBN: 978-1-64051-146-0

CONTENTS

INDEX OF ILLUSTRATIONS IN GREAT PICTURES AND THEIR STORIES

FOREWORD

Picture Study is rapidly becoming an important factor in education. "Nearly every progressive city," says the Bureau of Education, Washington, D.C., "is making use of some form of picture study in its school system."

The twentieth century has ushered in the reproduction of masterpieces in color! To what heights of delight the children of our schools may be carried by the famous pictures of the world in color!

It remains only for the elders to choose pictures adapted to the childish interests; pictures which will cultivate a taste for the best in art; pictures which through the impressionable early years will lead to a true understanding and appreciation of the world's masterpieces!

In preparing this series of readers it has been the aim of those selecting the pictures to consider always the child interest. The field of pictures is large. Not only have the "old masters" been drawn upon, but masters in modern art as well, including modern American artists. Thus constantly, through this series of pictures, the principles of beauty which made possible the "old masters" of yesterday are seen again in the art of today.

In the preparation of the text the child's interest and his ability to read are carefully considered. Real picture knowledge is conveyed in the child's own language.

In the primary grades the interest is largely in "what it is all about." Consequently the text aims to satisfy this curiosity, and at the same time lead to unconscious observation of those things which are most alive to the little child,—color, life, action.

The vocabulary for Books I, II and III is based on "The Reading Vocabulary," by

Horn, Horn, and Packer.*

In the intermediate grades, a lively interest in the story is always uppermost. Gradually an appreciation of picture-pattern develops. Simple elements in picture making,—i.e. center of interest, repetition of line and color, may be intelligently comprehended by children of the intermediate grades.

In the grammar grades great interest in the story continues, and with this interest there develops an appreciation of HOW the story is told, the real ART of the picture. The pupil not only learns that the picture is a masterpiece, but WHY. He thus acquires standards for judging other pictures.

Each picture is followed by a short sketch of the artist, told in a key adapted to the age and interest of the child.

The questions which follow the text will assist in developing an intelligent apprecia-

*See twenty-fourth Year Book, National Society for the Study of Education; Part I, 1925.

tion of the picture, and of the artist's work.

The author is particularly indebted to Miss Jennie Long, recently Supervisor of Primary Education, Peoria Public Schools, for valuable criticism of the primary text. Grateful acknowledgment is also made for the opportunity of practical work with a selected number of primary stories in the schools of Peoria.

The manuscripts of the intermediate and grammar grade books have been submitted to teachers of these grades, to whom the author is indebted for helpful practical suggestions.

The MUSICAL SELECTIONS for the pictures have been graciously contributed by Eva G. Kidder, Director of Music, Peoria Public Schools. The author believes this to be a very valuable feature of the text-book series.

THE AUTHOR.

ILLUSTRATED WITH REPRO-
DUCTIONS IN COLOR FROM
THE ORIGINAL MASTER-
PIECES, BY COURTESY OF
THE ART EXTENSION
SOCIETY OF NEW YORK.

MISS BOWLES
Wallace Collection, London

ARTIST: Sir Joshua Reynolds
SCHOOL: English
DATES: 1721-1792

LITTLE MISS BOWLES

Such a little girl! Such a little dog! They are having their pictures painted! This is little Miss Bowles and her new playmate a little black and white dog.

One day the father and mother of little Miss Bowles decided to have a picture of their little daughter. There were several artists living in London at the time, but Sir Joshua Reynolds was known as "the painter of children." So the father and mother decided that he should paint the picture of their little girl.

They invited him to dinner. Here he became acquainted with the little girl. He sat beside her at the table, and talked to her.

He told Miss Bowles so many things about his pets at home. He told her all about the other little girls that came to visit him. He told her many funny stories.

Very soon the little girl began to feel well acquainted with the artist. She thought him the kindest man she had ever known.

The next day she was delighted to go to the painter's studio.

Sir Joshua always kept many toys in his studio to amuse the children. He had birds, too, and a little black and white dog.

The tiny dog always made friends with the children. He liked to dance and frisk about. He liked to romp and play.

Of course as soon as the little girl appeared, out ran the little dog to greet her. She was delighted. They became good friends at once.

By and by when Miss Bowles sat for her picture, the little dog sat beside her.

How close she holds him! Oh, look! Her eyes are wide open and full of glee! She watches Sir Joshua as he works. She hugs the little dog close to her.

The little dog must be very uncomfortable. But he likes Miss Bowles so well that he is content to stay near her. His little black nose rests on her arm. His long black ear falls over her left hand. His eyes are wide open, too.

Miss Bowles wears a pretty light dress with a blue overdress. The blue ribbon on her hair matches the blue of her overdress. It matches the blue of her eyes, too.

See how the little dog's tail curves round, just like the little blue overdress curves round. Miss Bowles and her dog make a pretty pattern against the dark green background.

Sir Joshua had a beautiful garden about his house. Here we see a bit of distant blue sky. Nearer is the trunk of a sturdy old tree. Just back of Miss Bowles is a mass of dark green foliage.

The dark background makes the bright happy face of the little Miss shine out. It brings out the pretty colors in her dress. It brings out the dark and light in the coat of the little dog.

The little dog is very, very important. He helps to make the picture-pattern. His long back and tail make a line just like the other side of the picture. At the very tip-top where the two sides meet is the bright and happy face of little Miss Bowles!

THE STORY OF THE ARTIST

Many stories are told of the merry shouts of children's laughter that came from the artist's studio. Yes! Sir Joshua was the children's true friend!

When Sir Joshua was a little boy, he liked to draw and paint. At school he covered all his lesson papers with funny little sketches.

One day an artist came to town. He painted pictures of all the boys and girls. He made paper-cuttings of them, too. Joshua thought this was great fun. He, too, wanted to be an artist.

His father did not want him to be an artist. But by and by he said, "Joshua is a wonder; he must have lessons in drawing."

So Joshua went to the city of London to study. Later he began to paint children. He was one of the first of the great artists to paint children.

He made the children look so life-like and real that he was called "the painter of children," and as such he is now known.

SOMETHING TO TELL

1. Who is the little girl?

   Where is she sitting?

2. How does she look?

   How does she hold the dog? Why?

   How does the dog look?

3. Name the color of the dress.

   Overdress. Ribbon. Eyes.

   Name the color of the dog.

4. What is the shape

   of the picture-pattern?

5. Who is the artist?

   Can you name other pictures

   that he painted?

Related Music: SCHERZO .....*Beethoven*

Third Symphony.

MINUETTO WALTZ...

............*Chopin*

HEARING

From "The Five Senses"

"I found a shell upon the shore,
  I held it to my ear,
I listened gladly while it sang
  A sea song, glad and clear.

And that a little shell could sing,
  At first seemed strange to me,
Until I thought that it had learned
  The music of the sea."*

     —Rebecca B. Foresman.

"Hm-m-m-m-m-m-m—" sang the little shell. But never a secret would it tell!

"Hm-m-m-m-m-m-m—," still sings the little shell.

Oh, listen! The little girl wants to

*By permission of the author, Rebecca B. Foresman.

20

HEARING
(From "The Five Senses")

ARTIST: Jessie Wilcox Smith
SCHOOL: American
DATES: 1863-1935

hear the secrets of the sea, but the little shell only sings and sings.

Many times she has seen the water come rushing up on the shore. She has seen it run away again, too. Then she has picked up the pretty shells that were left on the beach.

"Hm-m-m-m-m-m-m-m

Hm-m-m-m-m-m-m-m." But never their secrets will they tell!

See the warm yellow sand of the beach. The green sea rolls right up to the shore. The patches of light make such a pretty pattern on the moving water!

See the whitecaps rolling in!

The little girl rests upon her knees. She leans with one hand upon the sand. With the other hand she holds the shell very close to her ear.

"Hm-m-m-m-m-m-m—

Hm-m-m-m-m-m-m—" But the sea will never tell its secrets!

The breeze is blowing. See! It blows back the little girl's hair. We can see her face. Her pretty blue eyes are wide open as she listens to the song of the shell. But try as she will, she cannot tell the words!

Oh, no! The sea will never, never, never tell its secrets!

Do you see the other shells lying near? There is young Mr. Turtle with a pink shell upon his back. All turtles do not wear pink shells. But this is such a pretty color on the warm yellow sand!

Mr. Starfish is there too. He is

lying on the flat of his back down near the front of the picture.

How pretty is the little pool of cool green water in the sand! It is just like a little mirror. Here and there about the shore, lie tangled bits of sea-weed.

Roll on! dancing whitecaps!
Roll on to the shore!
Bring sea-weed, bring shells
To my sandy door!

Perhaps we can make a picture like a little girl at the seashore.

Who will be the little girl? Who will hold the pretty shell to her ear? Perhaps you, too, may hear the beautiful music of the sea.

"Hm-m-m-m-m-m—Listen!

Hm-m-m-m-m-m-m-m." But not even to you will the little pink shell tell its story!

THE STORY OF THE ARTIST

The artist who painted our picture is called a "painter of children." She is an American. Her name is Jessie Wilcox Smith.

This artist always loved little children. You will be surprised to know where she learned so much about children.

In the kindergarten to be sure! Yes! Jessie Wilcox Smith was first a teacher in the kindergarten. She saw the children at their games. She saw them at their studies. She saw them dance and sing. She saw them laugh and play.

Oh, she learned so much about little children!

Later she began to illustrate fairy tales. She illustrated the story of "Jack and the Bean-stalk," "Little Lame Prince," "Babes in the Woods," and oh, so many more.

By and by she drew five pictures to illustrate the five senses. She called them, "Seeing," "Hearing," "Tasting," "Smelling," and "Touching." Our picture is "Hearing." Perhaps some day you may see the other four.

Later Jessie Wilcox Smith began to paint pictures of real children. Perhaps some day you may see some of her other pictures.

SOMETHING TO TELL

1. Have you ever heard the song
   of the shell?
   What does it say?
   Where did it learn its song?

2. What does the little girl hear?
   How does she look?
   What do you see on the shore?

3. What is the color of the beach?
   The water?

4. What makes the pretty pattern
   on the sea?

5. To what group does this picture
   belong?

Related Music: SONG OF THE SHELL..
                  ....*Dutch Folk Song*
                  THE SHELL ......*Parker*
                  HEARING..*W. O. Miesner*

DANCING IN A RING
Private Collection

ARTIST: Hans Thoma
SCHOOL: German
DATES: 1839-1924

DANCING IN A RING

What merry little children!
Eight little children
dancing in the ring.
Hand in hand they go!
Swinging merrily,
round and round,
to and fro.
The sky above!
The earth beneath!
And only the birds to hear them!

These little children live in Germany. They live in the country. They play all day in the bright clear sunshine.

See the gay colors they are wearing! Some are dressed in light. Some are dressed in dark.

The tallest girl wears a light dress.

Her feet are bare. See how she turns and looks around!

Her hair is long and curves across her back. See the pretty curves her arms make.

There are many curves in the picture. Can you find others?

See the little girl opposite in the dark green dress! She is swinging gaily to the music.

See the pretty curve she makes as she dances! See her dark red apron and yellow blouse!

They wear so many gay colors in Germany! They wear so many queer dresses in Germany!

Baby is here, too. She does not dance very much. Oh, no! She watches the feet of the other children. Soon she will go frolicking all over the meadow!

The artist knew how to arrange his "dark" and "light." He made a pretty pattern of "dark" and "light" against the yellow-green meadow.

See the little girl in the red plaid skirt! See the one in green! Red and green are pretty colors to put opposite.

Next the green dress is a purple one. The little girl has red stockings. They are as red as the red dress.

I see one little boy. He wears a light brown jacket. It has no sleeves.

He is having such a good time!

He likes to dance and play with these gay happy children.

In the far distance is a cool river. Beyond are soft purple hills. Above, is the clear, blue sky of Germany.

The colors in the river, the hills and the sky are very soft. The rolling meadow is a pretty soft background for the figures.

The happy peasant children in their gay-colored dresses make such a pretty pattern against the yellow-green background.

How happy are these merry little children! How they dance and sing! How they frolic about!

Round and round they go!
Hand in hand,
swinging merrily,
round and round
to and fro!
These happy children
dancing in a ring!

THE STORY OF THE ARTIST

This artist lived in Germany. He was born in the Black Forest in Germany. Here in the Black Forest he grew up with many other German boys and girls.

When he was a young lad he began to paint. But he did not paint on canvas!

Oh, no! He painted clock faces instead!

It was by painting the faces of clocks that this little German boy discovered he could draw and use the brush.

When he grew older he went to an art school. There he was taught drawing and painting. He continued to study for many years.

Later the little painter of clock faces became one of the great artists of Germany.

Hans Thoma painted many kinds of pictures. He painted landscapes. He painted children. Sometimes his imagination made beautiful pictures for him to paint.

Perhaps it was in the Black Forest that he saw these little peasant children dancing in a ring.

They wore so many bright colors. They made so many pretty curves as they danced. The artist put the curves and bright colors together and made a design. He kept the background simple so we could see only the happy children. Two, four, six, eight! Eight happy children dancing in a ring!

SOMETHING TO TELL

1. Where do these children live?

2. How many children are dancing?
   Name the colors in their dresses.
   Which are "light?"
   Which are "dark?"

3. What did the artist see
   as the children danced?
   What did he do?
   What did he make?

4. What do you like best
   about the picture?

5. Who is the artist?

Related Music: LASSIES' DANCE ....
                        ...*Swedish Folk Songs*
                AMARYLIS—*Old French*

ANGEL WITH A LUTE
Venice Academy

ARTIST: Vittore Carpaccio
SCHOOL: Italian
DATES: 1470-1522

ANGEL WITH A LUTE

An old fairy story says that it was long, long ago when people first learned to play on strings.

See our little player as she picks the strings!

See her thoughtful little face as she listens!

This is a big lute for the little musician. It has a pear-shaped frame: Across the flat surface run the strings. Its music is soft and low like a guitar.

Long ago beautiful pictures were painted for the churches. The people went to church to see the beautiful pictures. They read the pictures just as we read a book. They could read in a picture all the artist had to say.

All these pictures were very large. Many of the artists painted little angels in their pictures. Many times these little angels are standing at the bottom of the picture. Many times they are sitting upon steps.

Sometimes they are singing songs of praise. Sometimes they are playing upon musical instruments.

In one of these large pictures, painted so many years ago, is this beautiful child. She is playing upon a lute.

Our picture is only a part of a larger painting. It is so beautiful that it makes a picture by itself.

Here sits the little angel upon the beautiful marble steps.

See the pretty colors in the marble!

See how the light falls upon the steps!

The little player is beautiful. She sits with one leg thrown over the other, and her chin resting on the edge of the lute.

See her fingers as she picks the strings!

See the tip of her pretty head as she listens!

I think she is playing a hymn of praise to the beautiful saints in the picture above. We cannot see the saints. We see only a part of their robes. We see the folds of a red robe on the left. We see the folds of a gray robe on the right.

See the little player's light green robe! It falls over her lap. It wraps about her in a pretty fashion.

See how the light falls upon it! It makes clear, crisp edges on the pretty folds.

The blouse, too, has many folds. It is a pretty light red. It has wide sleeves with deep cuffs.

The artist made the blouse light red and the dress light green. He knew that red and green are always beautiful side by side. He made the colors light against dark.

See the pretty little face of the angel as she thinks and plays!

See the tip of her head as she listens to the music!

See the strength of her fingers as she picks the strings!

Do you think she ever looks at the sheet of music lying on the steps?

THE STORY OF THE ARTIST

Once upon a time a famous story-teller lived far across the ocean in Venice. This was over four hundred years ago. His name was Carpaccio.

He told wonderful stories. His stories were not printed in books. People did not write stories in books so long ago! His stories were painted in great pictures.

Carpaccio made beautiful story-pictures that all the people could read. In many of his pictures he painted gay, happy little people like our angel with the lute.

When Carpaccio lived, the artists were learning new things about painting every day. He was one of the first to understand how to paint the folds of clothing. He was one of the first to paint clear, crisp edges to his folds. If you look closely you will see that he has painted the robes of the angel in our picture in this way. This helps to make the picture beautiful.

Today many people go far across the ocean to see the story-pictures painted by Carpaccio. Though they were painted many hundred years ago, they are, today, among the great pictures of the world.

Our picture, "Angel with a Lute," hangs in a beautiful gallery in Venice. When the people go to see this picture they ride in a gondola right up to the door of the gallery. Can you tell why?

SOMETHING TO TELL

1. Do you ever play upon strings?
   Name a few stringed instruments.

2. What instrument is this?
   What is its shape?
   What kind of music does it make?

3. Where is the angel sitting?
   How does she look?
   What do you think about her hands?

4. How is she dressed?
   Where does the light fall?
   How did the artist paint folds?

5. Can you pose for a picture like
   our "Angel with a Lute?"

Related Music: ANGEL'S SERENADE.
.............*Braga*

A DISTINGUISHED MEMBER OF
THE HUMANE SOCIETY
National Gallery, London

ARTIST: Sir Edwin Landseer
SCHOOL: English
DATES: 1802-1878

A DISTINGUISHED MEMBER OF THE HUMANE SOCIETY

No dog had a greater record as a swimmer than the handsome Newfoundland, Paul Pry.

One day the English painter, Sir Edwin Landseer, saw the dog walking along the street. He carried a basket of flowers in his mouth. The artist had seen many Newfoundland dogs. He had painted them, too. But here was a wonderful specimen!

His coat was snowy white, his muzzle black except the tip of his nose. He was large and powerful.

Sir Edwin found the owner of the dog, and asked permission to paint his picture.

Next day the great Newfoundland

appeared at the artist's studio. His fine coat had been brushed until it was shining. At the master's command he leaped with one bound upon the table. Here he posed as we see him in the picture.

The artist pictured the dog as a member of a life-saving crew. He rests here upon a great stone pier at the water's edge. At a moment's notice he will leap into the water and be off.

The sea is all about him. A storm is coming up. We know this by the gray sky, and the whirling flight of the sea gulls.

See how gently the water laps against the stone pier! The cable of the mooring-ring floats upon its surface.

Brave and strong, the noble dog gazes out over the sea. His eye is keen for any need.

How strong is his body! See his chest and legs! See his powerful jaws!

His mouth is open. We can almost hear him breathe. His forelegs, hanging over the pier, show that he is alert and ready. His eyes are full of interest as they sweep the shore. The noble Paul Pry!

See how the light falls upon the fine white coat! It strikes full upon the broad white chest and the tip of the nose. How well the artist has painted the coarse white hair of the chest and back! How well he has painted the silken hair of the head!

47

The great Newfoundland fills the whole picture. We know he has a noble record. The artist shows the dog's intelligence. He shows his fearlessness. He shows his readiness to answer the call for help.

He is the noble Paul Pry!

THE STORY OF THE ARTIST

The artist, Sir Edwin Landseer, was a lover of dogs. He seemed to understand their thoughts. One day a lady asked him how he came to know so much about dogs. He said, "By peeping into their hearts, madam."

When our painter was a little fellow only five years old, he made wonderful sketches of animals. His father was an artist. He did all he could to help his little son. He sent the little Edwin to art school. He took him on many sketching trips. His father carefully kept all his little sketches.

The little Edwin had many pets of his own. Chief among them were three fine dogs. He named them Brutus, Vixen, and Boxer. He believed that animals were intelligent and could feel like human beings.

Edwin exhibited his first pictures when he was thirteen.

By and by he grew to be one of the greatest animal painters in the world. He is famous for his paintings of dogs.

All about his studio in London were

his pictures of dogs. Big dogs, little dogs, bloodhounds, Newfoundlands, and saucy little terriers.

One of his friends came often to the studio. Upon opening the door he would always call: "Keep your dogs off me!"

Landseer loved both wild and tame animals. He loved them so much that he would never hunt or shoot them.

When he went out in search of game, he carried a pencil instead of a gun. Instead of shooting his beloved animals he made drawings of them for his sketch book.

When he grew to be a famous artist, Queen Victoria of England made him a knight! Then he was called, "Sir" Edwin Landseer.

SOMETHING TO TELL

1. Have you ever had a pet dog?
   What was his name?
   What kind of a dog do you like
   best?

2. What kind of a dog is this?
   What are his points of beauty?

3. Where has the artist placed him?
   At what is he looking?

4. Do you like his coat? Why?
   What do you see in the dog's eye?

5. Who is the artist?
   How did he learn so much about
   dogs?

Related Music: CAPRICE.........*Ogarew*

CARNATION, LILY, LILY, ROSE
Tate Gallery, London

ARTIST: John Singer Sargent
SCHOOL: American
DATES: 1856-1925

CARNATION, LILY, LILY, ROSE

A pretty English garden in the twilight!

This is just the time to light the gay lanterns. Then the whole garden will be aglow!

Beautiful white lilies, carnations, and dark red roses grow in this garden. The little girls have hung their pretty Japanese lanterns all about the garden.

They hang upon the rose-bushes.

They hang upon the trees.

Now the two children have come into the garden. They are lighting the lanterns. Many of them already glow with a pretty warm light. They shine bright and gay in the quiet evening light.

See the little girl standing in the midst of the flowers!

Her dress is white. It is covered with a faint tint of twilight blue. It is almost the same color as the lilies.

The second little girl's dress is white, too.

See how the light shines upon their pretty faces as they look into the lanterns! Very soon, every lantern in the garden will be glowing orange.

Do you know that the white dresses and the white lilies make a pattern in the picture?

Begin with the white dress of the tall little girl. You will find that this same "white" swings round the picture.

It swings first to the dress of the

second little girl. Then up it goes to the lilies! Following lily by lily, round it goes, and comes back to the dress of the first little girl. This makes a pattern of white on the soft background of gray-green.

The lanterns, too, make a pattern. They, also, swing round the picture.

Often it is patterns like this in a picture that make it beautiful. An artist thinks very much about his pattern.

Do you see the dark color of the lanterns? Do you see the very dark flowers in the grass? This dark color was necessary. It helps to make a beautiful picture. How soft and gray is the green of the back ground! How graceful the pretty white lilies!

The little girls stand in the deep grass and flowers. They, too, are like pretty flowers in a garden. We want them to stay there always!

THE STORY OF THE ARTIST

This artist was born far across the ocean in Italy. His father and mother were Americans. So America claims him as one of her greatest painters. His name is John Singer Sargent.

The city where he was born is noted for its many wonderful picture galleries. These pictures were painted by the great artists of the world. This little boy liked to wander through the art galleries. He liked to study the beautiful pictures.

One day he went to the seashore. He

sat on the sand and began to draw a picture of the sea. A lady passed by. She saw him sketching with his pencil. She stopped to see his work. She saw that he had great talent.

"Why do you not paint your picture with colors?" she asked.

"Because I haven't any," replied the boy.

The lady went to the store. She bought a box of colors and gave it to the little lad. This was his first box of colors. Later he became one of the greatest painters in the world.

He lived a long time in England. It was in England that he saw this pretty garden. There are beautiful gardens everywhere in England.

After the picture was finished the

English people wanted to keep it in their country. They liked it for so many reasons. They knew that the children were little English girls. They knew the garden was an English garden. They liked the beautiful picture-pattern. They liked the warm and cool colors.

Then, too, they knew the artist had lived in England many years. There he had painted many of his famous pictures. So many of them had left England. Now they decided to keep this one.

So they placed it in their large picture gallery in London. Some day you may go to London. There you may see our beautiful picture—"Carnation, Lily, Lily, Rose."

SOMETHING TO TELL

1. Where is this pretty garden?
   What grows in the garden?

2. What time is it?

3. What are the little girls doing?
   Name one warm color.
   Name one cool color.

4. What is very important
      in every picture?
   What makes the pattern here?
   Why is some dark color used?

5. Who is the artist?
   Where did he live?
   Where may we see this picture?

Related Music: WILL-O'-THE-WISP
. . . .*Spross*

RETURN TO THE FOLD

Metropolitan Museum, New York

ARTIST: Anton Mauve
SCHOOL: Dutch
DATES: 1838-1888

RETURN TO THE FOLD

It is dusk. Evening is coming on. It is time for the sheep to return to the fold.

How stilled and hushed is the twilight! Not a sound is heard but the pat, pat, pat of the sleepy sheep as they tinkle homeward.

The old shepherd and his faithful dog lead the way. Soon the sheep will be under cover. Then their good friend, the dog, will lie down to rest.

See the long brown furrows of the plowed field! The fading light of evening has softened their edges. Their long lines lead straight off into the distance.

The shepherd walks beside the last furrow. The ground to the right has not been plowed. Here two deep tracks lead off toward the tall tree in the distance. Then they turn to the little light roof on the horizon.

How the sheep huddle together! Their backs make a big patch of light on the field. We can see only about ten sheep, but we know there are many more.

This artist had a way of his own to paint sheep. He always huddled them together. He painted a mass of light over all their woolly backs. He never drew all the sheep. He drew only a few, but these few tell us all about the others.

Do you see how the pale light of evening shows the roundness of their backs? The artist tells the whole story of their rounded backs by just letting the light play over their woolly surfaces.

This field must be near a wood for the long line of green trees march off into the distance. The "near" trees are tall. They become smaller as they disappear on the horizon. All the lines in the picture seem to go to the same spot. The furrows, the tracks, and the long line of trees all lead to the little light roof of the sheepfold. These long lines leading to the same place make the way seem very, very, long.

See the shepherd's figure! It is a sturdy dark pattern against the gray evening sky and dark field. He, with his faithful dog, has been out in the pasture all day. When evening came on, the watchdog, barking loudly and running here and there, gathered the flock together.

How the sheep huddle together!

See their woolly backs!

Now the dog, with his master, leads the little flock back over the field to the fold.

How proudly the dog walks along with the shepherd! He knows he has been a great help to his master.

On goes the shepherd and his trusty dog! On goes the pat, pat, pat of little feet!

Soon the shepherd, the dog, and the sleepy sheep will disappear. All will be in slumber. The stars, one by one, will come out, and throw a soft silvery light over the quiet field.

THE STORY OF THE ARTIST

It was in the low flat country of Holland that our painter, Anton Mauve, was born.

In Holland the wide fields and pastures stretch far to the distant horizon. All day long the cattle and sheep graze contentedly.

When Anton Mauve was little, he liked best to draw and paint. His parents, however, did not want him to be an artist. They had other plans for him.

The little lad knew what he wanted to do, so he kept right on with his drawing. By and by his father decided to give him drawing lessons. He studied hard for a long time.

Later he began to paint the fields

and pastures of Holland. He always drew sheep and cows in the fields.

Soon he became famous. It was his pictures of sheep that made him famous. Can you tell how he painted sheep?

He liked, also, to show the different kinds of light as it fell over the Dutch landscape and the woolly backs of his sheep.

Sometimes he painted morning light, sometimes afternoon light, and sometimes evening light, like the twilight in our picture.

Before very long, little Anton Mauve had grown to be one of the famous painters of Holland. Today his pictures hang in the greatest galleries of the world.

SOMETHING TO TELL

1. What time of day is it?
   Where is the sun?
   How do you know?

2. What makes the flock light?
   Are all the sheep carefully drawn?

3. Where are the sheep going?
   What lines in the picture lead
     to the same point?

4. Can you tell what makes the
     picture so still?

5. Who painted the picture?
   For what is he famous?

Related Music: NOW THE DAY IS OVER
   . . . . *Barnby*

   HE SHALL FEED HIS
   FLOCK—Messiah . . .
   . . . . *Handel*

   PASTORAL SYMPHONY
   —Messiah . . . . *Handel*

PILGRIMS GOING TO CHURCH

New York Public Library

ARTIST: George Henry Boughton
SCHOOL: English
DATES: 1834-1905

PILGRIMS GOING TO CHURCH

What a strange little company! This is a little band of Pilgrims on their way to church.

It must be early winter. A light snow covers the ground. The air is cold and gray. Perhaps the snowflakes will soon be falling.

See the pines! How still, and dark, and cold they are! When the wind blows they make a low moaning sound. They are still now. Everything is still. It is so still that only the light footsteps of the Pilgrims can be heard. Hush, hush! They do not speak, except in whispers. No one is in sight. Not even a dog, a rabbit, or a bird is seen.

Some of the Pilgrims carry guns. There may be an unfriendly Indian hiding behind a tree. The red man has sharp arrows. The white man must carry a gun to protect the women and children.

See where the artist has placed the armed men! There are two leading the little band. Two are in the rear. Another walks in the center with the women and children.

This is the first little band to pass this way. Another is coming. We see the first man of the second band.

See how the Pilgrims are dressed! They wear warm colors. They are the same colors as the trees and woods among which they live.

The men wear high hats and large white collars and cuffs. They wear short trousers and coats with belts.

The women wear long dresses and capes. They wear little bonnets and white kerchiefs about their shoulders. Sometimes they wear white aprons, too.

The pretty dark colors of the Pilgrims' clothes make a sharp contrast against the white snow. This helps us to see their figures better.

See the picture-pattern the artist made!

He placed the big tree trunks so they divided the picture into pretty spaces. He made one large space. He made three smaller spaces.

In the large space is a very important group, the minister, the women, and the little girl.

See the light in their faces!

See the light on the tree trunks! The trees stand tall and straight like the Pilgrims.

Soon many little Pilgrim bands just like the one in our picture will gather in their little church for worship.

These sturdy pioneers were very thankful for all their blessings. They set one day apart for a day of thanksgiving. This was our first Thanksgiving Day. Now we have a Thanksgiving Day every year.

Can you tell the month in which Thanksgiving Day comes?

On Thanksgiving Day we always think of the Pilgrim fathers. We think of their trials and hardships. We remember how brave they were. We, too, are thankful.

THE STORY OF THE ARTIST

The artist who painted our picture was born in England. His name is George Henry Boughton. He came to America when he was three years old. When he grew older he started to school. In school he learned to draw and paint. This was his delight!

He would rather draw and paint than do anything else. While the other boys were playing baseball, football, and taking part in other sports, George liked to sketch.

One day he planned to go fishing. He went into a store to buy hooks and a line. Instead, he came out with a box of colors!

When he grew older he went to England to study. Later he became famous for his paintings of early American life.

When he was a little fellow he listened to the stories of the Mayflower, Plymouth Rock, and the Pilgrims. We are not surprised that as he grew older he painted pictures of the early American days.

Not only did he paint pictures of these early days, but he wrote stories as well and illustrated them with his own drawings.

"Pilgrims Going to Church," is one of his best known pictures. When we look at this painting we may learn much about the life of the Pilgrims. We like the picture because it tells us about these early days. We like it because it is a beautiful picture.

SOMETHING TO TELL

1. What is the season of the year?
   What kind of a day is pictured?

2. Who is the little band?
   Where are they going?
   Why are they so quiet?

3. Describe the men's dress.
   Describe the women's dress.
   Name the colors in their clothes.

4. What special day did the
      Pilgrims name? Why?
   Do we celebrate this day? Why?

5. Why do you like this picture?

Related Music: THANKSGIVING HYMN
                ....*Elvey*
                OLD HUNDREDTH ......
                ....*Bourgeois*, 1551
                O, GIVE YE THANKS—
                ....*Mozart*

GOING TO CHURCH IN MORAVIA
Private Collection

ARTIST: Josef Uprka
SCHOOL: Czechoslovakian
DATES: 1861-1940

GOING TO CHURCH IN MORAVIA

What funny little people! Who are they? Where are they going?

They are going to church. They are going to church dressed in their very best clothes.

This is the Sabbath Day. The men and women of the village have dressed in their finest clothes to go to church.

What strange costumes! Surely this is not America. Of course not. These strange costumes do not belong in America. They belong to a people who live in a distant land far over the sea. This land is Moravia. These people live in the country. They are called peasants.

One day the artist, who lived in Moravia, was out in the country. He caught sight of this procession of peasants on their way to church. They looked like great birds moving across the green earth.

The sun, shining on their gay costumes, dazzled his eyes. All he could see was a bright pattern of red, white, and yellow against a background of green.

Against this background the peasants made a pattern like a triangle. We see the two in the "near" part of the picture first. Then we follow the red caps up to the back line of figures walking across the picture. Then down we come, to the first figures again.

Do you see that the first woman carries a prayer book? The others do the same. The artist painted the first figures very carefully. Then he knew we would understand how the others were dressed.

See the red bonnet of the first woman! See the long ties! See the balloon sleeves! See the yellow skirt with the red spots!

The man is a big strong fellow. He goes proudly stepping along. He wears a little hat trimmed with flowers. Sunday is his holiday.

See the red collar and big sleeves! See the gay yellow handkerchief hanging from his belt! No wonder the artist's eye was dazzled by this gay troop of peasants!

See the bright warm sunshine!

The sun must be high in the heavens for the shadows are very short. They make cool blue-gray patches on the bright green field.

Bright, dazzling sunshine is everywhere!

These happy peasants do not mind the sunshine. They work in the fields all the day long. Their skin is burned to a deep brown.

When the Sabbath Day comes the women don their gay holiday dresses of red, white, and yellow. The men, too, wear their best clothes, and little hats trimmed with real flowers. All dressed in their Sunday best, they parade across the green fields to the village church.

What a picture they make!

No wonder the artist's eye was dazzled by the sight!

THE STORY OF THE ARTIST

This artist knew the country people of Moravia well. He was born in Moravia. His name is Josef Uprka.

Though Uprka has traveled and studied much, he likes best to live in his own country among his peasant friends. Here he likes to paint the great out-of-doors, the scenery of his native land.

He also likes to paint the peasants at their work or play. At their labors he pictures them in their working clothes. At play he pictures them in holiday dress.

The lively color in the peasant's holiday dress pleased the artist's fancy. He liked to see their gay colors sparkling in the sunshine.

He painted his peasant pictures of Moravia in every season and every time of day. His favorite hour is noon, when the red, yellow, and green of the costumes are ablaze in the sunlight. Then shadows are short. When shadows are short, they make only little patches of cool color in a picture. Then all the rest of the picture is filled with bright warm sunlight.

It was just about the noon hour that the artist saw this gay parade of peasants in our picture!

Uprka still lives in Moravia. He is the leader of a group of painters who are giving all their time to painting true pictures of the sunlight and color of their native land. How wonderful it is to paint out-door pictures!

SOMETHING TO TELL

1. Where do these people live?
   Where are they going?
   What time is it?
   How do you know?

2. Name the colors in the woman's dress.
   Describe her bonnet. Her sleeves.

3. Name the colors in the man's dress.
   Describe his hat. Shirt. Collar.

4. Explain the picture-pattern.
   What makes the colors sparkle?

5. Who is the artist? Where does he live?

Related Music: COME LET US BE JOY-FUL ....*Mozart*

THE PRIMITIVE SCULPTOR
Private Collection

ARTIST: E. Irving Couse
SCHOOL: American
DATES: 1866-1936

THE PRIMITIVE SCULPTOR

A bit of soft clay. The gentle, sure touch of the Red man. And lo! A little rain god!

Soon the Indian sculptor will have two little rain gods. These he will carry to a near-by spring. He will place them about the spring as a prayer for water.

With a plentiful supply of water his cares will vanish completely. He will have an abundant crop!

Here squats the kindly red man. See him as he models the little figure! A touch here, a touch there, and soon the face of the little image appears.

The red man's face is filled with kindly interest as he watches the image grow.

See his thoughtful eyes! The expression of his mouth tells that he is thinking carefully as he works. A gentle touch here, a gentle touch there, and the little rain god appears!

See the fine curve of the Indian's head against the dark background. See the long curve of his back. How broad and massive are his shoulders! See the sinewy arms and the strong hands as they model the little image!

The Indian is a fine figure against the dark background. The dark background brings out the pretty color of his skin.

He is not the warrior Indian. He is not a fighter. He is an Indian of today. He lives much as the Indians lived before the white man came.

His blue-black hair is parted and hangs in long braids before his shoulders. The braids are bound in gay colors of green and yellow. Pretty leaves of light green and yellow fall from his head. They follow the curve of his back.

See the heavy buckskin leggings! They are a warm soft yellow.

He wears moccasins covered with beads. They are doubtless made by the Indian himself. The Indians always plan their own designs and weave the beads into beautiful patterns. These moccasins are woven into a pretty pattern of white, green, and red. And he wears gay colors,—this red man of the Pueblos.

Before him is an Indian jar. It is

made of clay and burned to a dark red. It is painted with colored clays. Some one has made an Indian design upon its surface. The background of the design is the same color as the buckskin leggings.

Beside this jar is another. It is as dark as the Indian's blue-black hair. The artist repeats his colors again and again. This helps to make the color-pattern of his picture.

Beyond is the low red light of a slow fire. A long lazy line of green rises against the dark background. Perhaps you can find where the red color of the fire and the green color of the lazy line are repeated in the color-pattern.

Below on the ground are patches of dark and light. There before the

Indian sits one little rain god! What a queer little image he is! He has a funny round face. He has short arms and legs. And see the red patch of paint on his cheek!

There he sits with a little Indian jar in his arms, waiting for the second little rain god.

Soon the second little image will be finished. He, too, will have a funny little nose and a patch of red paint on his cheek. Then together they will go, the Indian and the little rain gods to the near-by spring. The red man will chant a prayer to the Great Spirit. He will ask for water.

By and by the rain will descend!

A plentiful rain means an abundant crop for the red man!

THE STORY OF THE ARTIST

The artist loves to paint Indians, because he knows the red man well.

His name is E. Irving Couse. He has lived long among the Indians of New Mexico. Here also live many other artists.

These Indians are not fighters. They are peaceful red men. In the early days they would not allow an artist to paint their pictures. They were afraid their souls would return and dwell in the pictures, instead of going to the happy hunting ground. Now it is different. Gradually the Indians have become more and more willing to pose for their pictures.

This artist and the Indians are on the best of terms. You will be surprised to know that the gay green sweater of the artist caught the eye of the red man. It said just one word to him. That word was "green." Then, too, the artist was a very large man. This, also, said just one word to the Indian. That word was "Mountain." So they gave him a new name! They called him "Green Mountain!"

Today Green Mountain is known as the good friend of the red man. The Indians come often to his house to visit him. They are always willing to pose for the artist's pictures. It is his paintings of the American Indian that have made this artist famous.

Today his pictures hang in the most important galleries in America and are greatly admired.

SOMETHING TO TELL

1. Where does this Indian live?
   What is his tribe? Is he a warrior?
   What is he doing? Why?

2. Name the color of his skin. Hair.
   Are these colors repeated? Where?

3. What kind of leggings does he
      wear?
   What kind of moccasins?
   Name their colors.
   Where are they repeated?

4. Why does an artist repeat his color?

5. Do you like the dark background?
      Why?
   Who is the artist?
   For what is he famous?

Related Music: FROM AN INDIAN
                        LODGE .....*MacDowell*

PRONUNCIATION OF PROPER NAMES

BOUGHTON ....(bô' tōn)

CARPACCIO .... (kär pät' chō)

COUSE .... (kouz)

LANDSEER .... (lănd' sēr)

MAUVE .... (mōv)

REYNOLDS .... (rĕn' ŭlds)

SARGENT .... (sär' jĕnt)

THOMA .... (tō mạ)

UPRKA ...... (ōō' pr kä) Rolled R

SUGGESTIONS TO TEACHERS

STUDYING THE PICTURE. Any picture presented for study becomes more interesting when freely discussed in a natural way by the class. Before reading the text it is always advisable to study the picture. Pupils should be encouraged to give their own impressions; tell what they like in a picture, and WHY they like it.

In the primary grades the story interest is uppermost—"What is it all about?" By tactful questioning the teacher may bring out many artistic points for observation. She may speak of color and action as well as story content. She may lead the pupil to discover new words which will appear in the text. These may be emphasized, written upon the board and studied. Thus they are greeted like old friends when met in the story.

DRAMATIZATION. In the primary grades many pictures lend themselves to dramatization. With little children the "acting out" of the picture is a real joy. Under no circumstances is it necessary to burden one's self with an EXACT reproduction in the class room. The details of costume are not required. Any outstanding accessory, however, easily at hand, may add interest. It is the EFFORT on the part of the child to reproduce the pose and action that is of value. Frequently, if time permits, children may take turns in posing, letting the class decide who does best. Thus in a simple and direct way, many of the pictures selected for primary study may be given an added interest and charm.

CORRELATION. Language lessons both oral and written may be based on the work in Picture-Study. The questions following each picture, when answered either orally or in written form, necessitate close observation and intelligent expression.

As far as possible, each child should own his own pictures. This leads to the making of picture-study books, envelopes, folders, calendars, and other simple projects which utilize and also preserve the pictures.

The music hour offers still another opportunity for related study. Pictures, like music, create emotions. When possible in the study of pictures, add the music which may suggest the spirit and atmosphere of the picture. THE INTEREST IS ALWAYS KEENLY STIMULATED WHEN PORTIONS FROM VARIOUS SELECTIONS ARE PLAYED, AND THE CHILDREN PERMITTED TO CHOOSE THE ONE BEST SUITED TO THE PICTURE.

The suggestions for musical selections which follow the questions on the picture will be of great value to the teacher.

www.ingramcontent.com/pod-product-compliance
Lightning Source LLC
LaVergne TN
LVHW010309070426
835511LV00021B/3457